SCIENCE FOR KIDS

SPACE

God's Majestic Handiwork

SCIENCE FOR KIDS

SPACE

God's Majestic Handiwork

Illustrated by Susan Windsor

iCR

INSTITUTE FOR CREATION RESEARCH

Dallas, Texas
ICR.org

SCIENCE FOR KIDS

SPACE

God's Majestic Handiwork

First printing: October 2017
Third printing: November 2020

All Scripture quotations are from the New King James Version.

ISBN: 978-1-946246-03-5
Library of Congress Catalog Number: 2017953518

Please visit our website for other books and resources: ICR.org

Printed in the United States of America.

Table of Contents

This Incredible Universe

* *God created the universe in six days.*
* *He made the sun, moon, stars, and planets on Day 4.*
* *The universe is about 6,000 years old.*

Our silver moon gently lights the night sky. Our blazing sun keeps time better than a clock. Our home planet has every feature needed to support life. And all three work in perfect harmony for our good. Where did all this order and beauty come from?

The Bible says God spoke this incredible universe into being by the power of His Word. "All things were made through Him, and without Him nothing was made that was made"

Day 1: Light

Day 2: Separation of Waters

Day 3: Dry Land

(John 1:3). In other words, if it exists, God created it! And according to the Bible's timeline, God created everything in six days about 6,000 years ago.

On Day 4 He made the sun, moon, stars, and planets:

> Then God said, "Let there be lights in the firmament of the heavens to divide the day from the night; and let them be for signs and seasons, and for days and years; and let them be for lights in the firmament of the heavens to give light on the earth"; and it was so. (Genesis 1:14-15)

Day 4: Sun, Moon, Stars

Day 5: Sea Animals and Birds

Day 6: Land Animals and Humans

Outer Space and the Bible

✳ *God created the heavens and the earth.*
✳ *God made the sun, moon, and stars to give us light and track time.*
✳ *God stretched out the universe.*

Did you know the Bible's very first verse mentions space? "In the beginning God created the heavens and the earth" (Genesis 1:1). Earth is the planet we live on—I'll bet you already knew that! Space, called the "heavens," includes our sky filled with birds and clouds. Outer space, filled with distant planets and stars, is also part of the heavens.

According to Genesis 1:14-18, God put the sun, moon, and stars in space to give us light and help us track time. People use the sunrise, sunset, phases of the moon, and Earth's orbit around the sun like giant clocks to tell days, months, and years.

Job 9:8 says, "[God] alone spreads out the heavens." God stretched out the whole universe! Is it still stretching? Most scientists think so.

The Bible doesn't tell us everything there is to know about space. But we can trust anything it does say—including who made it and how it works.

Smart Guys from the Past

* *Famous scientists made some great discoveries about the universe.*
* *Many believed they were studying God's laws and wonders in creation.*
* *We continue to build on their discoveries today.*

People once believed the earth was the center of the universe. They thought all the planets and stars orbited Earth—even the sun! A guy named **Claudius Ptolemy** (TOL-uh-mee) invented a complicated theory on how he thought the planets and sun moved around Earth in circles called epicycles. Though Ptolemy's theory matched some scientific observations, it wasn't right.

Ptolemy
(About 100–170 A.D.)

Nicolaus Copernicus challenged the idea of epicycles and an Earth-centered universe. He looked at the planets and stars, made calculations, and realized that the planets orbit the sun instead. His ideas made some people angry.

Copernicus
(1473–1543)

Johannes Kepler discovered the three laws of planetary motion that helped astronomers accurately predict planets' positions in our solar system.

Kepler (1571–1630)

Galileo Galilei helped the world realize that Copernicus was right. Galileo constructed a telescope and used it to discover some of Jupiter's moons. Finding moons orbiting Jupiter showed that everything didn't orbit Earth as people commonly believed.

Galileo (1564–1642)

Isaac Newton found a way to calculate a planet's orbit. He also discovered the three universal laws of motion and conducted important research on the nature of color and light.

Newton (1643–1727)

Albert Einstein figured out how gravity relates to space and time. He also made many scientific predictions that were proved right long after his death.

Einstein (1879–1955)

How Big Is Our Universe?

* *The universe is so huge that we can't see the end of it.*
* *Astronomers use large measuring units for distances in space.*
* *Our special planet is one tiny part of the universe.*

The universe is the biggest thing there is because everything, everyone, and every place fits inside it. Just how big is it? Astronomers believe the universe is at least 550,000,000,000,000,000,000,000,000 miles! And there could be even more to it than we can detect.

How do scientists express such enormous distances? Instead of writing super-long numbers in miles, they measure in astronomical units, light-years, and parsecs.

If we could take a rocket ship far into outer space, we'd see that our sun and nearby planets form only a tiny part of the Milky Way galaxy. And the universe has billions of galaxies. Our special Earth is like one grain of sand on a giant sandy beach.

- One astronomical unit = 93 million miles
- One light-year = 5.9 trillion miles
- One parsec = 19 trillion miles

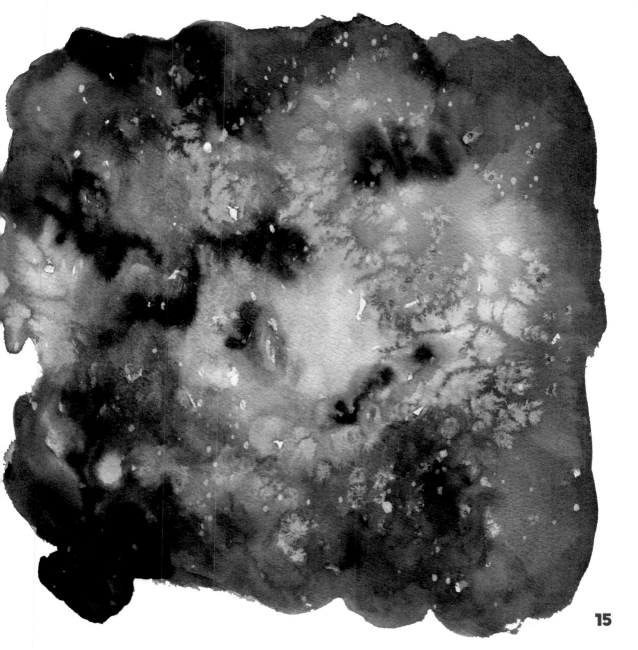

What Is the Big Bang?

✳ *Some people think the universe started with a huge explosion.*
✳ *This doesn't match the Bible's account or scientific evidence.*
✳ *Explosions don't organize—they destroy.*

Have you ever dropped your math book and found that the math problems solved themselves? Have you ever spilled a bottle of paint and it created an exact copy of the famous *Mona Lisa*? If you threw your laundry into the air, would it land neatly sorted into folded shirts, pants, and shorts? We never see chaos accidentally organize objects, do we? Well, surprisingly, some scientists think it's possible for total accidents to create magnificent order.

These scientists believe a giant explosion—called the Big Bang—created the universe almost 14 billion years ago. But explosions create chaos and destroy. Our universe displays order and balance—it doesn't look blown up into existence at all.

In the 1920s, astronomer Edwin Hubble saw signs the universe may be expanding, and some think this is a leftover effect from the Big Bang. But even if the universe is growing after its creation, that doesn't necessarily require a Big Bang.

Big Bang vs. Bible

✳ *The Big Bang is not part of the Genesis creation account.*
✳ *The Big Bang and the Bible do not agree.*
✳ *The Bible wins every time.*

The Big Bang says the universe began in a fiery, chaotic explosion of space, time, energy, and matter that came from nobody-knows-where. But the Bible says it began with water that God commanded into being.

The Big Bang says stars formed over long periods of time as a result of the explosion. But Genesis 1:16 tells us God made stars on Day 4 of the creation week.

The Big Bang story says everything formed over billions of years. But the Bible's beginnings tell of only a six-day creation just thousands of years ago.

If the Big Bang were true, that would mean living creatures died for millions of years *before* humans ever existed. But the Bible says death began *after* Adam and Eve sinned.

The Big Bang and the Bible cannot both be true. And the Big Bang's got big problems. So, when it's the Bible vs. the Big Bang, the Bible wins every time.

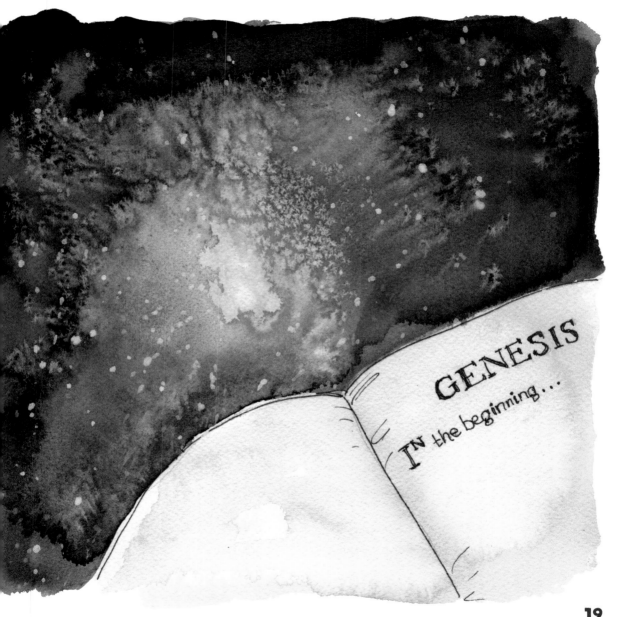

GENESIS

IN the beginning...

Big Bang vs. Science

* *No one has proved the universe started with the Big Bang.*
* *The Big Bang doesn't match scientific evidence.*
* *We don't need the Big Bang to explain the universe.*

Scientific evidence does not support the Big Bang. In fact, hundreds of scientists signed a public statement rejecting the Big Bang because it requires too many made-up explanations to fix its weaknesses.

One of these made-up explanations is called inflation. Supposedly, right after the Big Bang the universe had a huge growth spurt. But even some scientists who don't believe the Bible admit that inflation doesn't fit the evidence very well.

If the Big Bang were true, it would have created equal amounts of matter and something called antimatter. But there's very little antimatter in the visible universe.

We don't need the Big Bang to explain how this incredible universe came into being. Our awesome Creator accomplished it just by the power of His Word.

Far-Out Fact: The Big Bang scientific model has made almost no accurate predictions. Instead, it has been tweaked to agree with observations after the fact.

Our Solar System

✳ *Anything that orbits the sun is part of the solar system.*
✳ *Our solar system shows amazing design.*
✳ *Eight planets call it home.*

It's a beautiful day in the neighborhood—Earth's neighborhood, that is! Eight planets call this solar system home. And so do all other celestial objects that orbit the sun, including asteroids, comets, centaurs, dwarf planets, trans-Neptunian objects, and dust.

Our sun is amazingly stable for a star. It doesn't flare or pulse like other stars. And when solar flares do happen, they are not big enough to destroy life on Earth.

The four rocky planets—Mercury, Venus, Earth, and Mars—orbit closest to the sun. They're also

Mercury   Venus   Earth   Mars   Jupiter

known as terrestrial planets. Earth's the biggest.

The four gas giants—Jupiter, Saturn, Uranus, and Neptune—orbit farther out. They're made of a rocky core enclosed by gases held together by gravity. Some also contain ice.

Pluto used to be called the ninth planet, but scientists found many similar-size rocks orbiting with it. Since Pluto's so small, they renamed it a dwarf planet instead.

God created our solar system with incredible balance, order, and design.

Now, let's get to know these amazing citizens in Earth's neighborhood!

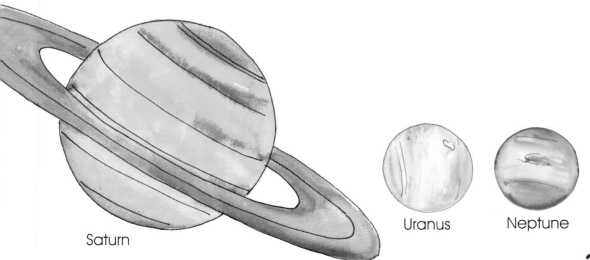

Saturn

Uranus

Neptune

Sun

✴ A bright star burning near the center of our solar system.
✴ All the planets, asteroids, and comets orbit around it.
✴ God put the sun in just the right spot to support life on Earth.

God made all the stars—including me—and I get to rule the day! I give heat and light to everyone on Earth. In fact, I release more energy every second than a billion cities could use in a year!

I love mornings—no need for coffee for me! Each day, I can't wait to burst over your horizon in the east. Though it looks like I move across the sky, your planet actually rotates around me.

Living things need my energy to survive. I burn at the best distance from Earth and brightness for people, plants, and animals to thrive. If I were any farther away, you'd freeze. If I were closer, you'd sizzle.

Well, I've enjoyed our chat, but it's getting late. I'm headed west, my friend. See you in the morning!

Far-Out Fact: Our sun is so big that it makes up more than 99% of the mass in our solar system.

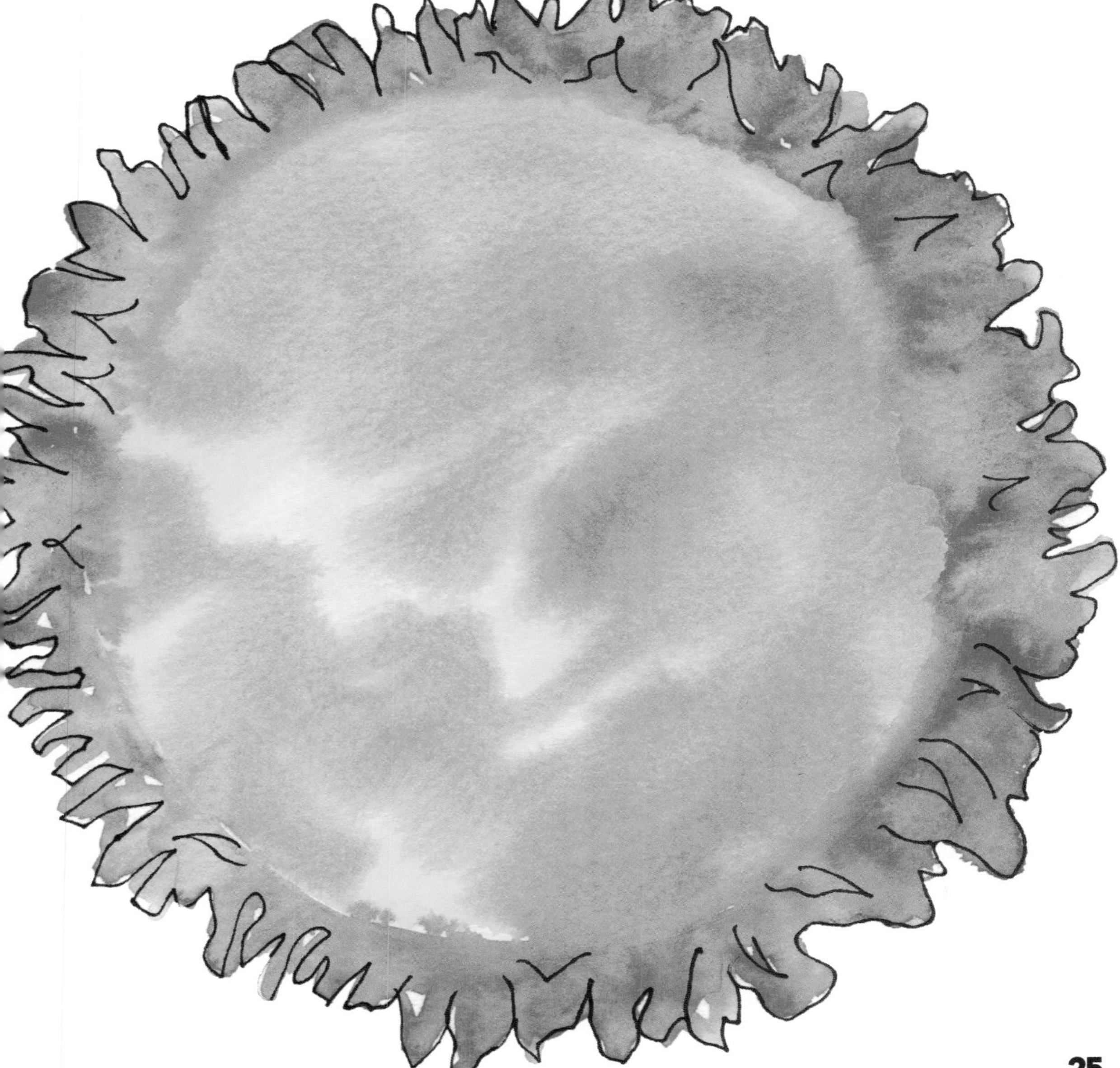

Mercury

* *The closest planet to our sun.*
* *It boasts a speedy orbit and extreme temperatures.*
* *This rocky, cratered ball looks similar to our moon.*

Hey, it's me—Mercury! I zip around the sun at over 100,000 miles per hour! That's awfully quick, if I do say so myself.

Orbiting so close to the sun gives me some wacky weather! Every day brings me fever. I get up to 800°F—hotter than Earth's scorching deserts. But at night I get the chills! At -290°F, I'm colder than Earth's fiercest winter.

You don't need a telescope to see me—just look in the sky at the right time! From Earth, I look like a twinkling star. But up close, my surface has valleys, mountains, plains, and lots of craters.

I'm just a baby compared to the age many scientists give me. My magnetic field would have decayed long ago if I were billions of years old. But it's still going. That's one way you can tell God made me just several thousand years ago!

---

* Diameter: 3,032 miles
* Length of day: 4,222.60 hours
* Distance from sun: 36,000,000 miles
* Orbital period: 88 Earth days
* Average temperature: 332°F
* Number of moons: 0
* Ring system? No
* Global magnetic field? Yes

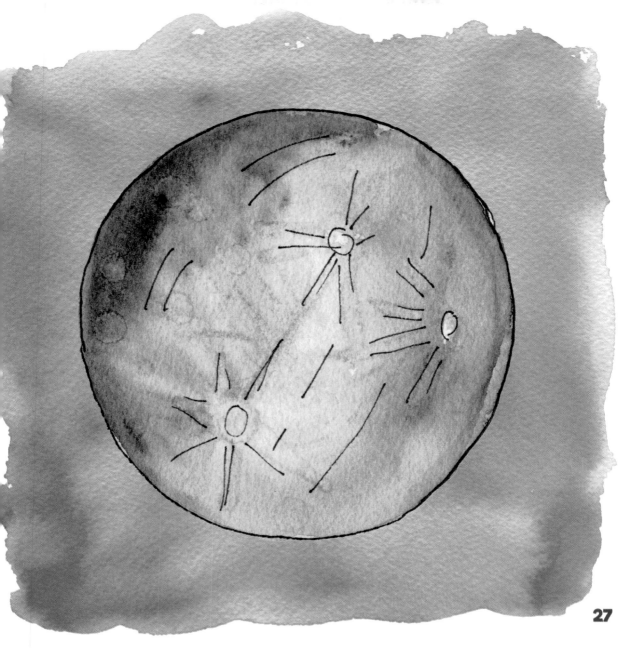

Venus

* *Venus is called Earth's sister planet.*
* *It has a scorching-hot atmosphere both day and night.*
* *It spins backward.*

Nice to meet you—I'm Earth's sister planet, Venus. Like many siblings, we share some common traits. Earth and I are made of rock, not gas. And we're about the same size—almost twins!

But if you take a closer look, you'll see we have huge differences, too. While Earth overflows with life, I'm hot and hostile. Super-thick clouds made of poisonous gases trap heat within my atmosphere, so my scorching surface is impossible for anyone to live on.

I rotate clockwise, while most of the other planets spin counterclockwise. If the universe started with a Big Bang, scientists would expect to see all planets in our solar system turning the same direction. But that's not what happens! God created each of us with His own design in mind.

---

* Diameter: 7,521 miles
* Length of day: 2,802 hours
* Distance from sun: 67,200,000 miles
* Orbital period: 224.7 Earth days
* Average temperature: 867°F
* Number of moons: 0
* Ring system? No
* Global magnetic field? No

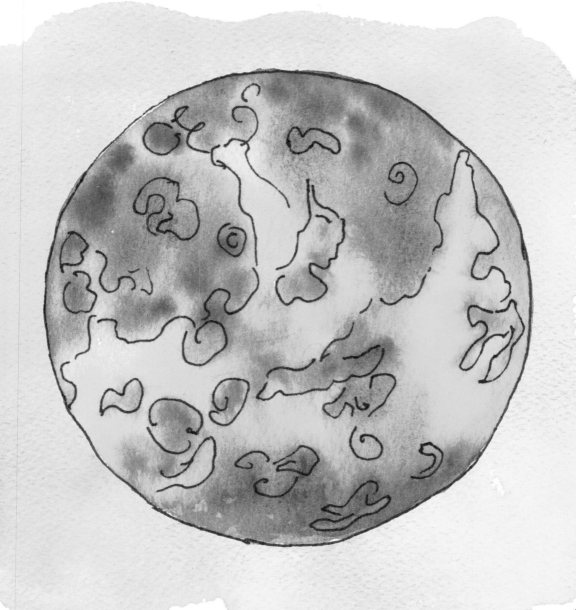

Earth

✳ *Our home sweet home.*
✳ *Made of rock, it orbits as the third planet from the sun.*
✳ *It's the only known planet that can support life.*

I'll skip the introduction—you and I know each other pretty well. But after all the years we've spent together, you may have forgotten just how special I really am.

I am your home in the universe, specially created for your life and joy!

Some call me a Goldilocks planet because everything about me is juuust right for life. I'm not too hot and not too cold because of my just-right distance from the sun. I tilt at a good angle to create seasons. My ideal temperatures enable water to remain in liquid form in most parts of my surface. And our Creator made me juuust right for humans to see His glory.

My mountains, rocks, oceans, and trees—and the living creatures dwelling throughout them—reveal God's kindness, power, and creativity each and every day.

- Diameter: 7,926 miles
- Length of day: 24 hours
- Distance from sun: 93,000,000 miles
- Orbital period: 365.2 days
- Average temperature: 59°F
- Number of moons: 1
- Ring system? No
- Global magnetic field? Yes

Moon

✳ *A rocky, cratered ball that orbits around Earth.*
✳ *It reflects sunlight and supports life on Earth.*
✳ *Its movement shows it could not be billions of years old.*

Hidey-ho, neighbor! I'm your marvelous moon. I reflect the sun's rays to help you see at night. But God made me to be much more than just a jumbo-size nightlight. As I travel around Earth, my gravity pulls on its oceans, causing the tides to come in and go out.

I've been inching away from Earth a tiny bit each year. If this were happening over billions of years, I would've started out too close to Earth for life to exist. But since I've only been around for several thousand years as the Bible says, I've probably only moved a few hundred feet. That small change is no big deal.

Big Bang scientists think I formed when a planet-size object collided with Earth long ago. They say broken rocks supposedly came together to make me and put me in the perfect orbit. But that's silly! How could an accident make me so ideal for life on Earth? A smart Creator with a grand plan is a much better explanation.

Mars

✳ *The most Earth-like planet in the solar system.*
✳ *It's not friendly to life.*
✳ *Scientists plan to someday send a manned spacecraft to Mars.*

Little green men and spaceships? Sorry, friends. That's only in the movies. People used to think that intelligent creatures like humans might live on me, the Red Planet. But after sending small unmanned spacecraft for a visit, scientists know it's just my two moons and me.

I have some features similar to Earth's—mountains, canyons, volcanoes, and even icy places on my north and south poles. My days last around 24 hours, and I experience a lot of the same kinds of weather. But I don't have enough oxygen to support life or a magnetic field to protect you from the sun's charged particles. If you ever visit me, you'll need to solve these dangerous problems.

Rumor has it that astronauts aim to land on my surface within the next 20 years. Perhaps I'll see you soon!

- Diameter: 4,221 miles
- Length of day: 24.7 hours
- Distance from sun: 141,600,000 miles
- Orbital period: 687 Earth days
- Average temperature: -85°F
- Number of moons: 2
- Ring system? No
- Global magnetic field? No

Jupiter

* *A gigantic planet where storms, moons, and rings come in super-size!*
* *Jupiter's Great Red Spot is a raging hurricane.*
* *The planet's got so much heat on the inside that it must be young.*

Thank you, thank you! I humbly accept this year's Planet of Enormous Size award. This trophy means so much. (Sniff, sniff.)

I'm a giant ball of gas that turns to liquid around my rock core. Strong winds wrap me in colorful clouds, creating dark "belts" and light "zones" that dazzle. My buddy the Great Red Spot is a hurricane about the size of Earth! It's been raging around me for years and probably won't stop anytime soon.

If I were billions of years old, they'd call me Mister Cool. But I release nearly twice the energy I receive from the sun! Since God made me only thousands of years ago, my still-steamy insides make me the King of Heat Street.

---

* Diameter: 88,846 miles
* Length of day: 9.9 hours
* Distance from sun: 483,800,000 miles
* Orbital period: 4,331 Earth days
* Average temperature: -166°F
* Number of moons: 69
* Ring system? Yes
* Global magnetic field? Yes

Saturn

* *A favorite yellow gas-ball planet with shiny rings of ice.*
* *Its rings face an onslaught of attacks from natural forces.*
* *Saturn's moon Enceladus (en-SEL-uh-dus) is icy on the outside and full of energy on the inside.*

I'm famous for my icy rings and sandy yellow color. Who am I? Why, Saturn, of course!

My delicate rings face ruthless enemies—gravity, meteorite impacts, and other forces threaten to destroy them. If they had confronted such foes over billions of years, they'd be merely an icy memory. But they still surround me and shine like new.

I'm the only planet known to have Trojan moons. That means some of my moons orbit in different positions along the same path and at the same speed.

One of my moons, Enceladus, has enough energy inside it that it forces its southern pole to spew out icy particles. Big Bang scientists struggle to explain how such a tiny moon could still have this energy after billions of years.

---

* Diameter: 74,897 miles
* Length of day: 10.7 hours
* Distance from sun: 890,800,000 miles
* Orbital period: 10,747 Earth days
* Average temperature: -220°F
* Number of moons: 62
* Ring system? Yes
* Global magnetic field? Yes

Uranus

* *A sky-blue planet made of gases and ice.*
* *No one knew it was a planet until 1781.*
* *Surrounded by thin, icy rings, Uranus rotates on its side.*

No one can say I follow the crowd. I like to get a different view of the universe as I roll sideways around the sun. At 1.78 billion miles away, I'm 19 times farther from the sun than Earth. That's why it takes 84 Earth years for me to orbit just once!

In 1984, creation physicist Dr. Russell Humphreys predicted my magnetic field's strength using a biblical timescale of 6,000 years for my age. A couple of years later, the *Voyager 2* probe's measurements proved him right.

No one knew what I was until William Herschel discovered me with his telescope in 1781. But if you know where to look, you can see me with your eyes on a very dark night. I may not be the most famous planet, but that's all right by me. I have my own special features that show off God's power and the truth of His awesome recent creation.

- Diameter: 31,763 miles
- Length of day: 17.2 hours
- Distance from sun: 1,784,800,000 miles
- Orbital period: 30,589 Earth days
- Average temperature: -320°F
- Number of moons: 27
- Ring system? Yes
- Global magnetic field? Yes

Neptune

✳ *A sky-blue ball of ice and gas.*
✳ *The most distant planet in our solar system.*
✳ *Its heat is a clue to its youth.*

If you search for me through your telescope, you'll see a tiny blue ball of ice and gas. I'm your cold buddy, Neptune! Hydrogen, helium, and a bit of methane wrap around my icy core. The methane creates my blue hue.

Voyager 2 spacecraft's 1989 photos of me caught scientists by surprise! I'm surrounded by five major rings of ice and more moons than they could see from Earth. My largest moon, Triton, has a "retrograde orbit"—that means it moves in the opposite direction of my spin.

You can call me Mr. Freeze, but deep down inside I'm super hot! If I were billions of years old, that sizzle would have fizzled a long time ago. But high temps make perfect sense for a young planet like me.

Far-Out Fact: French mathematician Urbain Le Verrier used math equations—not a telescope—to discover Neptune.

- Diameter: 30,775 miles
- Length of day: 16.1 hours
- Distance from sun: 2,793,100,000 miles
- Orbital period: 59,800 Earth days
- Average temperature: -330°F
- Number of moons: 14
- Ring system? Yes
- Global magnetic field? Yes

Pluto, the Dwarf Planet

✳ *A little ball of rock orbiting three billion miles away from Earth.*
✳ New Horizons *took the dwarf planet's first glamour shots.*
✳ *Pluto's smooth surface gives us clues about its age.*

Hellooooo! Can anyone hear me? It's Pluto. I'm cold and lonely way out here.

For years, they said I was one of nine planets in the solar system. But after they found many other small rocky objects like me, they gave me a new title: dwarf planet!

The *New Horizons* spacecraft launched from Earth in 2006 to visit me. The trip took nine years! The craft captured close-up photos of my smooth, heart-shaped plain—called the Tombaugh Regio after the man who discovered me.

If I were billions of years old, my surface should have lots of craters from collisions with other space objects. But I don't have many craters at all! Since God made me only thousands of years ago, I haven't had time to earn more battle scars.

- Diameter: 1,464 miles
- Length of day: 153.3 hours
- Distance from sun: 3,670,000,000 miles
- Orbital period: 90,560 Earth days

- Average temperature: -375°F
- Number of moons: 5
- Ring system? No
- Global magnetic field? Unknown

Magnetic Fields

* *Invisible shields that deflect charged particles from space.*
* *They have limited life spans.*
* *Their strength today shows they have only existed for thousands of years.*

Magnetic fields are space superheroes! They surround many planets and moons in our solar system. Earth's is like an invisible shield protecting us from harmful charged particles.

But magnetic fields can't pack a powerful punch forever! They constantly lose energy like a flashlight's battery when it's left on too long. And as far as we know, these magnetic field "batteries" don't get a recharge.

Even superheroes have their limits—magnetic fields can't hang on for millions of years. So, why do Mercury, Earth, Jupiter, Saturn, Uranus, and Neptune still have them? They must be only thousands of years old like the biblical timeline indicates.

Far-Out Fact: Physicist Russell Humphreys correctly predicted the magnetic strength of several planets using a Bible-based 6,000-year estimate of the universe's age.

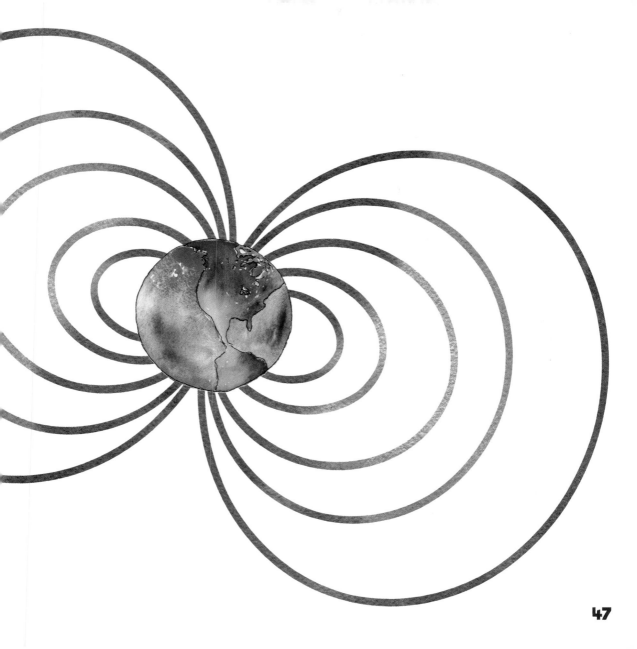

Moon Lighting

✳ *The moon spins at the same rate it orbits Earth.*
✳ *We only see one side of the moon from Earth.*
✳ *The moon cycles through eight phases each month.*

The moon rotates once every 27 days. So, why do we only see one side of it from Earth? This is because the moon spins at exactly the same rate it orbits our planet. The same side is always turned toward us. Even so, the visible side of the moon looks different depending on the amount of sunlight that reaches its cratered surface. It cycles through eight phases throughout the month.

When the moon orbits on the opposite side of Earth from the sun, it appears large, round, and well-lit. This phase is called a full moon. When the moon orbits between Earth and the sun, it looks completely dark. This phase is called a new moon. The illustration on the next page shows all of the moon's phases as it transitions from a new moon to a full moon and back again.

The moon waxes when it shines brighter each night, moving toward a full moon phase. The moon wanes when it turns darker, moving toward a new moon phase.

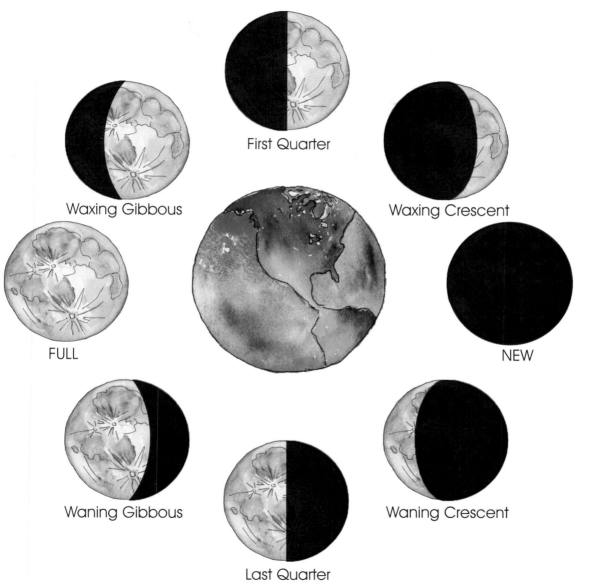

First Quarter

Waxing Gibbous

Waxing Crescent

FULL

NEW

Waning Gibbous

Last Quarter

Waning Crescent

Star Search

* *Stars are balls of burning gas.*
* *Three kinds of stars are red dwarfs, yellow dwarfs, and giant blue stars.*
* *Blue stars show the universe can't be very old.*

Have you ever looked up in the sky on a dark night, away from city lights? The heavens twinkle with countless bright balls of burning gas—you know, stars. Though they may look the same from Earth, stars actually come in different sizes and colors.

The coolest stars are red dwarfs. They're the most common stars we find.

Yellow dwarfs are a little hotter and keep a pretty stable temperature and brightness. Our sun is a yellow dwarf, and it has the ideal features to support life on Earth.

Blue stars are the hottest and burn brightest, which means they run out of fuel the fastest.

Blue stars can only last one or two million years—not billions. And they're all over the universe! With so many blue stars still burning bright, how could the universe be billions of years old?

The Bible says that "one star differs from another star in glory" (1 Corinthians 15:41). We see these words ring true as we study the amazing variety of stars.

Far-Out Fact: Many other types of stars shine in the night sky—including giants, supergiants, and white dwarfs.

"He Made the Stars Also"

✶ *The Bible says God made the stars (Genesis 1:16).*
✶ *Big Bang scientists say stars form on their own.*
✶ *Natural star formation theories ignore the laws of physics.*

Big Bang scientists think new stars form from collapsing gas clouds and then replace old stars. They call these supposed star-formation areas star nurseries. But are there really little star babies appearing out of nowhere?

Well, the funny thing is, no one has actually seen a star being born. There's no evidence for it, and natural star formation goes against the laws of physics. Gas expands—it doesn't collapse.

When gigantic stars run out of fuel, they produce a powerful explosion called a supernova. Only the star's "guts" and a few leftover pieces remain. Less massive stars' cores collapse more gradually after they explode and then form a nebula (gas cloud). Supernovas and nebulas create colorful designs in space.

Scientists can't agree on how stars formed. But the Bible reveals the secret. It says God made the heavens and the earth. And "He made the stars also" (Genesis 1:16).

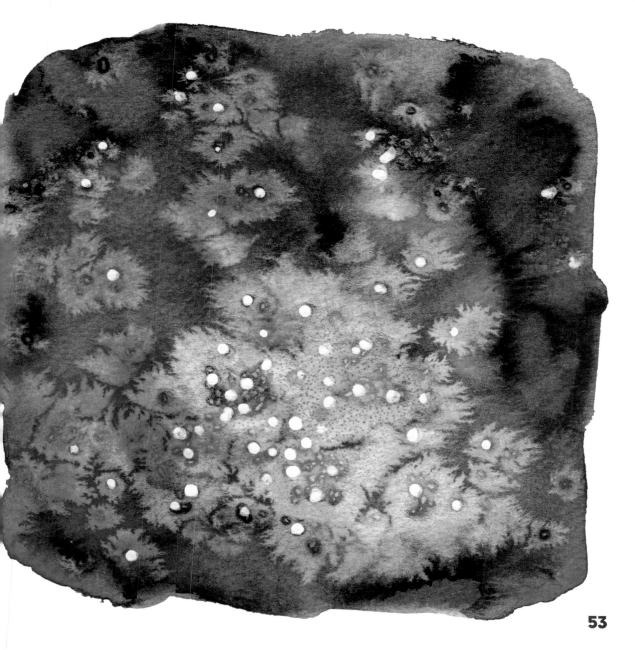

Mapping the Sky

* *A constellation is a group of stars used to form an imaginary picture.*
* *People use them to map the sky.*
* *They represent animals, mythological creatures, people, or objects.*

For thousands of years, people have imagined pictures in the stars called constellations (kon-stuh-LAY-shuns). Constellations provide an easy way to map the sky. You may have seen or heard of the hunter Orion, Little Bear, Andromeda (an-DROM-eh-da), or Cassiopeia (kass-ee-uh-PEE-ah). The International Astronomical Union recognizes 88 official constellations. About half were listed by the Greek astronomer Claudius Ptolemy.

The hunter Orion constellation is illustrated on the next page. Blue stars make up Orion's belt. People see some different constellations depending on what part of the world they live in and what time of year it is. Orion is visible above Earth's equator where everyone around the world can see it.

Far-Out Fact: Smaller patterns of stars within a constellation are known as asterisms (AS-tuh-riz-uhms). The Big Dipper is an asterism, not a constellation. It's part of Ursa Major (the Great Bear).

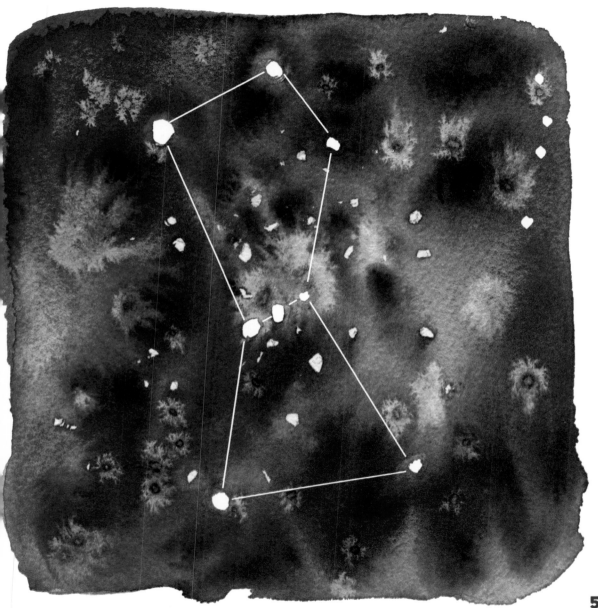

Distant Starlight

* *The Bible says stars' light reached Earth on the same day God created them.*
* *The speed of light doesn't seem fast enough for starlight to reach Earth in a day.*
* *But there are many ways God could have accomplished this.*

Light moves fast. Scientists use sensitive instruments to measure light's round-trip speed of 186,000 miles per second.

Some stars are so far away that it seems their light would take billions of years to reach us, even moving that fast. But it couldn't have taken billions of years since the Bible says stars gave light to the earth the same day God created them (Genesis 1:15).

So, how did distant starlight reach us so quickly? Creation scientists have

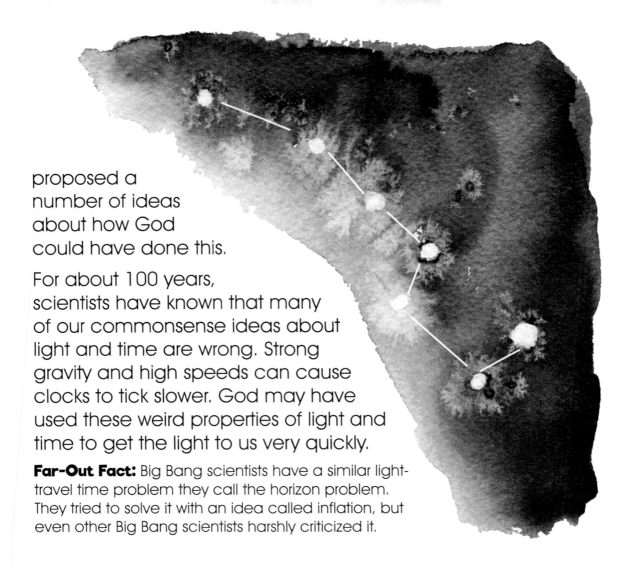

proposed a number of ideas about how God could have done this.

For about 100 years, scientists have known that many of our commonsense ideas about light and time are wrong. Strong gravity and high speeds can cause clocks to tick slower. God may have used these weird properties of light and time to get the light to us very quickly.

Far-Out Fact: Big Bang scientists have a similar light-travel time problem they call the horizon problem. They tried to solve it with an idea called inflation, but even other Big Bang scientists harshly criticized it.

Star of Bethlehem

✳ *A unique star that shone in the night sky when Jesus was born.*
✳ *Wise men in the East followed the star to find Jesus.*
✳ *The star's appearance was likely a supernatural event.*

If you're familiar with the Christmas story in the Bible, you probably remember the wise men who followed a star to find Jesus.

> The star which they had seen in the East went before them…and stood over where the young Child was. (Matthew 2:9)

The wise men saw a bright star they had never seen before. What was it? Some say it was a planetary conjunction—where two or more planets come so close together they look like one really bright star.

But a planetary conjunction doesn't move quickly enough or closely enough to hover over an earthly location. More than likely, the appearance of the Bethlehem star was a supernatural event. Since it moved and then stood still, we know it was a unique guiding light—a special star God used to lead people to His Son, Jesus.

Asteroids and Comets

* Asteroids and comets orbit the sun.
* Comets are balls of dirt and ice, and asteroids are chunks of rock.
* Comets support a young universe.

Millions of small, rocky objects called asteroids orbit the sun. Their orbits usually run between Mars and Jupiter, so that area is known as the asteroid belt. Asteroids are mostly made of carbon, silica, or metal.

Most asteroids completely burn up when they enter Earth's atmosphere and can look like falling stars. Some large asteroids could cause damage. But none are expected to hit Earth in our lifetime.

Comets are like dirty snowballs. They orbit the sun in a path shaped like a squashed circle. They spend most of their days traveling far out in space. But when they draw near the sun's scorching heat, some of their ice turns to gas and trails like tails behind them!

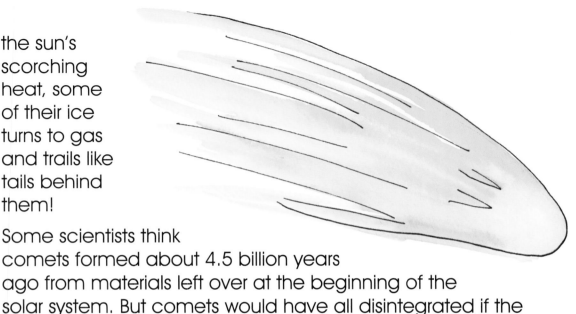

Some scientists think comets formed about 4.5 billion years ago from materials left over at the beginning of the solar system. But comets would have all disintegrated if the universe were even just millions of years old.

To believe in a super-old universe, Big Bang scientists must explain how these dirty snowballs could still exist. They claim that after comets go dark and can't be seen anymore, new comets replace them from the Kuiper (KY-per) Belt and Oort (OHRT) cloud. But the orbits of many comets (such as Halley's Comet) are very different from the orbits of objects in the Kuiper Belt. Also, no telescope can see the Oort cloud, so it may not even exist!

Far-Out Fact: At the rate a comet loses material every time it orbits the sun, most couldn't last more than 100,000 years.

Gabbing about Galaxies

* *A galaxy is a gigantic system of stars, gas, and dust held together by gravity.*
* *Galaxies are grouped by their shape.*
* *Astronomers estimate the universe has at least two trillion galaxies—and probably more.*

Have you ever heard of the Milky Way? That's the galaxy you live in if you're reading this book from Earth!

Each galaxy fits into one of three groups based on its shape: elliptical, spiral, or irregular.

Elliptical galaxies have black holes at their centers and are made up of stars pulled toward each other by gravity. Together, they form a slightly squashed circle. The stars are often close together, making elliptical galaxies look like one bright giant star from a distance.

Spiral galaxies like our Milky Way look like a bicycle wheel with curved spokes. They often have black holes at their centers, too. These black holes may help anchor the surrounding stars with their super-strong gravity.

Irregular galaxies include any galaxy not shaped like an elliptical or spiral. Whatever the design, we know God placed each star in each galaxy right where He wanted it!

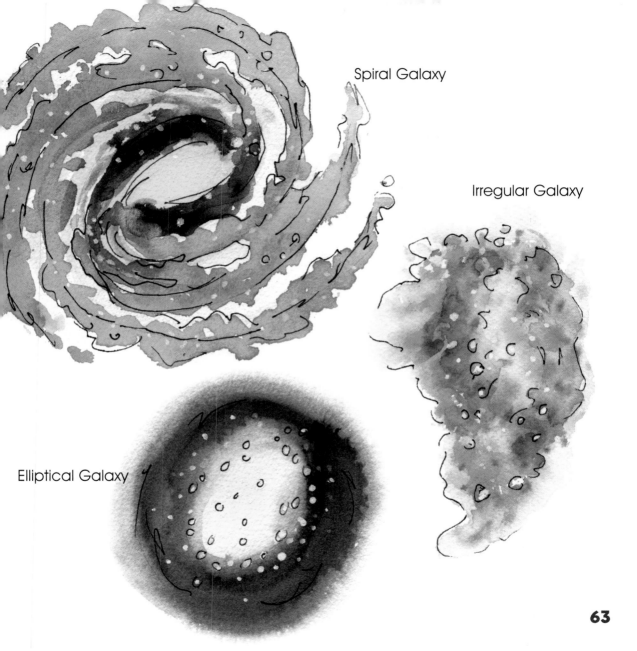

Spiral Galaxy

Irregular Galaxy

Elliptical Galaxy

63

Mysterious Black Holes

* *Black holes can form from extremely large collapsing stars.*
* *They swallow anything that comes near them.*
* *They hover at the center of many galaxies.*

Black holes aren't scary, but they can seem a little mysterious. A black hole is an area of space where the gravity is so strong that even nearby light can't escape—so the hole stays dark all the time.

What causes black holes? Since they're found at the centers of spiral and elliptical galaxies, God probably created them during creation week. But black holes can also form when big stars, like giant blue stars, run out of fuel.

When they can't hold themselves together any longer, the big stars blow up. The star's outer layer creates a colorful supernova remnant. And the remaining star stuff collapses into a super-small space and becomes a black hole. The once-giant bright star squishes down into a space so small that it could fit on the head of a pin!

Far-Out Fact: The supermassive black hole at the center of our Milky Way galaxy is called Sagittarius (saj-i-TAIR-ee-uhs) A*.

Strange and Wonderful Things

* *The countless wonders in our universe reflect God's diverse creativity.*
* *The more we explore space, the more mind-boggling things we learn!*
* *Scientists still find new celestial objects and features that don't fit natural explanations.*

God filled our universe with some strange and wonderful stuff!

Eclipses have fascinated people for thousands of years. As far as we know, Earth is the only planet that experiences a total solar eclipse where the moon completely covers the sun. Lunar eclipses occur when Earth blocks the sun's light from reaching the moon.

Did you know that many stars are found in pairs? Known as **binary stars**, they orbit each other.

Massive points of light called

quasars (KWAY-zars) are the brightest objects in the universe and may be powered by **black holes**.

Small chunks of rock and debris called **meteoroids** fly through space. When they enter a planet's atmosphere, they become **meteors**—or shooting stars. They create a streak of light as friction with the atmosphere heats them. Once they hit the ground, they're **meteorites**.

When solar particles strike Earth's magnetic field, colorful light streams called **auroras** appear in the sky near the North and South Poles. Auroras in the north are often called the aurora borealis (boar-ee-AL-is) or the northern lights. Auroras near the South Pole are referred to as the aurora australis (aw-STRAY-lis) or the southern lights.

Our Young Universe

* *Big Bang scientists claim the universe is billions of years old.*
* *The Bible's timeline shows the universe could only be thousands of years old.*
* *Much evidence confirms the Bible's young age for the universe.*

Many people like to say that the universe is old, but that's not what the Bible says! The Bible says God created everything in six days. The timeline in the Bible adds up to about 6,000 years. And we can trust what the Bible says because God inspired it.

Science also confirms it.

We've talked about some evidences for a young universe throughout this book, but let's check out some more!

Sunlight is breaking down a chemical called methane in the atmosphere of Saturn's moon Titan. All of the methane should be gone after millions of years, but it's still there!

A thick layer of dust would have collected on Saturn's icy

rings after billions of years. The rings must not have been there for very long—they sparkle and shine.

Like Jupiter, Neptune gives off more heat than it receives from the sun. After billions of years, it should have exhausted its heat, but it hasn't. It must be young.

Jupiter's tiny moon Io has lots of erupting volcanoes. These eruptions require lots of energy—energy that should've been used up if Io is billions of years old.

Evidence of still-erupting volcanoes was recently discovered on Venus. Even Big Bang scientists admit that Venus' surface looks much younger than it should if Venus is billions of years old.

History of NASA

* *The U.S. government established the National Aeronautics and Space Administration (NASA) in 1958.*
* *NASA is one of the largest space programs in the world.*
* *NASA's projects have furthered space exploration.*

1958–1963 NASA's Project Mercury aimed to put a man in space. Alan Shepard was the first American in space. John Glenn was the first American to orbit Earth.

1961–1966 Project Gemini (JEM-in-eye) involved longer missions, spacewalking, and learning to dock with other spacecraft.

1961–1972 Project Apollo sought to put a man on the moon before 1970. Neil Armstrong and Buzz Aldrin achieved this goal in 1969.

1962–2015 NASA launched many space probes to explore new worlds. They gathered photos and information for all eight solar system planets plus dwarf planet Pluto.

1972–2011 NASA's Space Shuttle program used rockets to launch manned spacecraft and to put satellites like the Hubble Space Telescope in orbit around Earth.

1973–1979 NASA helped build an Earth-orbiting research lab for the U.S. and Europe. Known as Skylab, it fell back to Earth in 1979.

1993–Present NASA co-sponsored construction and maintenance of the International Space Station (ISS). The ISS orbits Earth with crew members from the U.S. and other nations.

Far-Out Fact: NASA's next big goal is to send astronauts to Mars.

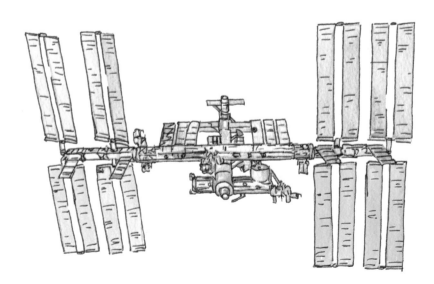

Hubble Space Telescope

✳ *The Hubble Space Telescope orbits Earth.*
✳ *Named for astronomer Edwin Hubble, NASA launched it in 1990.*
✳ *It takes millions of incredible space pictures.*

Light from Earth's cities and towns hinders what we can see in the night sky. And Earth's atmosphere blurs images from space. Thankfully, the Hubble Space Telescope orbits Earth above all this light pollution and lets us see much farther into space than telescopes on the ground can.

The Hubble uses an eight-foot mirror to focus a camera and take pictures of stars and galaxies. The first mirror didn't work very well, and scientists had to make "space glasses" (little mirrors) to help Hubble see better. Once astronauts put the space glasses on the Hubble, it could see farther into space than any telescope ever before!

The Hubble's space pictures changed the way we view and understand the universe. Scientists plan to launch an even better telescope in the future to replace the Hubble. What other works will we see declaring God's awesomeness?

Far-Out Fact: Scientists control the Hubble Space Telescope from the ground, and solar panels keep it powered.

Space Probes

✳ *A space probe is an unmanned craft used for space exploration.*

✳ *Probes gather information about planets, moons, comets, and asteroids.*

✳ *They often collect evidence for a young universe.*

Space probes are spacecraft that explore the solar system without an astronaut on board. They're loaded with gadgets and sensors to gather information about whatever object they're exploring. Interplanetary probes fly by planets, moons, comets, and asteroids. Orbiters revolve around a planet or moon to map and study its surface. And as you might guess, landers land on and explore the surface.

The chart below lists some of the most groundbreaking space probe missions.

- *Mariner 2* (1962)—Interplanetary, the first probe to study another planet—Venus.

- *Voyager 1 & 2* (1977)—Interplanetary, *Voyager 1* went to Jupiter and Saturn; *Voyager 2* went to Neptune and Uranus.

- *Galileo* (1989)—Orbiter, studied Jupiter and its moons.

- *Cassini* (1997)—Orbiter, in Saturn's orbit since 2004; dropped the *Huygens* lander on Titan's surface.

- *Spirit* (2003)—Lander, Mars rover explored the planet's surface.

- *New Horizons* (2006)—Interplanetary, flew by Pluto.

Spirit

Space Shuttles

* *NASA hosted the Space Shuttle program for 30 years.*
* *They built five shuttles.*
* *NASA is shifting into a new stage of space travel and exploration.*

NASA's Space Shuttle program ran from 1972 to 2011. They built five shuttles: *Columbia, Challenger, Discovery, Atlantis*, and *Endeavour*. These partly reusable spacecraft couldn't travel to the moon. But they could transport astronauts, supplies, and equipment into Earth's orbit to work on the Hubble Space Telescope or board the International Space Station.

Many people gathered to watch rockets launch the shuttles at the Kennedy Space Center in Florida. But space travel comes with great risk. The *Challenger* and *Columbia* shuttles had disastrous technical problems during their final missions. No one on either crew survived.

Since the last shuttle flight in 2011, NASA astronauts have been riding with Russian cosmonauts to the International Space Station. But NASA plans to launch astronauts in their new Space Launch System rocket and the Orion spacecraft.

Far-Out Facts

Kick back. Relax. Enjoy more far-out facts!

The sun rotates on its axis about once every 27 days.

Although Mercury orbits closest to the sun, Venus' thick clouds make it the hottest planet.

Mars' Olympus Mons is the largest volcano in our solar system. It's three times bigger than Earth's Mt. Everest.

The universe has more stars than there are grains of sand on all the beaches and deserts on Earth.

Mathematically, a white hole could exist in space, but nobody has found one yet.

Voyager 1 discovered dark rings of dust and rock surrounding Jupiter. Unlike Saturn, we can't see Jupiter's rings with an Earth-based telescope.

Pluto is smaller than Earth's moon.

So far, the International Astronomical Union recognizes four other dwarf planets besides Pluto: Ceres (SIR-eez), Haumea (how-MAY-uh), Makemake (MOCK-ay-MOCK-ay), and Eris (EHR-is).

The asteroid belt runs between Mars and Jupiter and contains over a million asteroids.

Planets discovered outside our solar system are called exoplanets. So far, we've discovered over 2,000 of them—each one unique.

Twelve people have walked on the moon.

Apollo 17 astronaut Eugene Cernan scratched his daughter's initials in the lunar dust.

An electrical issue during their mission threatened to keep the Apollo 11 crew from returning home. Buzz Aldrin solved the problem using a felt-tip pen.

The Hubble Space Telescope only takes pictures in shades of black and white. Astronomers usually add color before releasing the photos.

Footprints in Moon Dust

✳ *The U.S. and Russia competed in a space race.*
✳ *Astronauts landed on the moon in 1969.*
✳ *Six more moon missions followed.*

Have you ever run in a race? Well, how about a space race? In the 1960s, the United States and Russia were competing to see who could send a man to the moon first. Both countries built spacecraft that carried astronauts in orbit around the earth. They also sent probes to take pictures and explore the moon.

Finally, in 1969, the Apollo 11 mission landed on the moon's rocky surface. U.S. astronaut Neil Armstrong dropped his boots into the moon dust and said, "One small step for man, one giant leap for mankind." Pilot Buzz Aldrin joined him 20 minutes later. Together, they explored the new world, gathered moon rocks, and left an American flag.

In later years, six more manned spacecraft rocketed to the moon. Apollo 13 reached orbit but didn't land. Through these missions, we learned many things about our cratered neighbor.

Far-Out Fact: Since the moon has no wind or weather, the astronauts' footprints are still in the dust!

Becoming an Astronaut

* *Astronauts must have a bachelor's degree in a science or math field.*
* *They must be U.S. citizens and meet height/weight requirements.*
* *They must have experience suited for this challenging, adventurous career.*

Would you like to be an astronaut? Well, you'll need to work hard in school and go to college. Choose to study one of the STEM disciplines—science, technology, engineering, or math. After you earn your degree, get your pilot's license. You'll need 1,000 hours of experience flying a plane.

NASA recruits adventurous people! Show that you can go out and experience new things. Learn a musical instrument, hike through the Teton mountains, or study a foreign language. To be an astronaut, you must be between 62 and 75 inches tall. This is short enough to fit in a rocket but tall enough to reach the controls. You'll also need to be in excellent physical condition for the rigors of space travel.

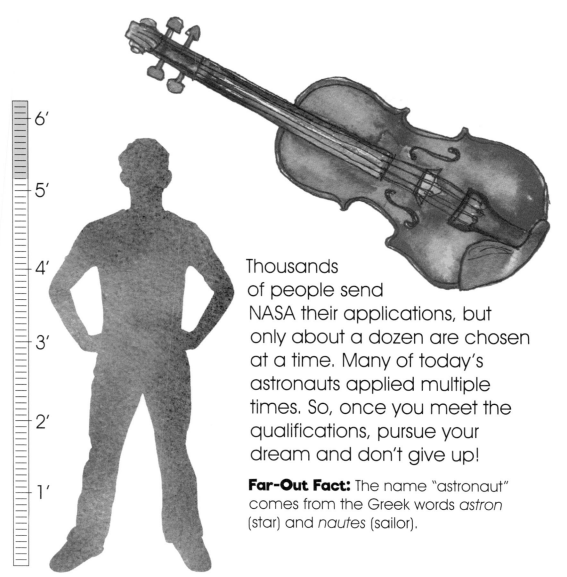

Thousands of people send NASA their applications, but only about a dozen are chosen at a time. Many of today's astronauts applied multiple times. So, once you meet the qualifications, pursue your dream and don't give up!

Far-Out Fact: The name "astronaut" comes from the Greek words *astron* (star) and *nautes* (sailor).

Human Body in Space

✳ *When people go into space, they have to bring Earth's supplies.*
✳ *Spacesuits provide protection, air, and Earth-like pressure.*
✳ *Space has strange effects on the human body.*

God created Earth with the perfect conditions for humans to live. No one knows another place in the universe like it. So, when astronauts go into space, it's pretty dangerous. There's no oxygen to breathe, and the sun's rays are scorching hot. Space has no gravity or atmospheric pressure and no food or water!

Living in space does strange things to the human body.

Height: In space, astronauts grow an inch or so taller!

Heart: Astronauts' hearts pump less and get smaller.

Balance: Without gravity, astronauts lose their sense of balance. They have to use their other senses to stay upright.

Bones and Muscles: Astronauts use specialized exercise equipment to slow muscle and bone loss.

Eyes: Astronauts' eyeballs change shape. This may happen because of increased pressure in their brain and spinal fluid. They take different pairs of glasses to correct their vision during the mission.

Savvy Satellites

* *A satellite orbits around Earth or another celestial object.*
* *Man-made satellites gather information or provide communication.*
* *The moon is a God-made satellite because it orbits the earth.*

About 1,100 active man-made satellites orbit Earth above us. Each receives signals from Earth and sends signals back.

How did these satellites get up there? Governments and companies launched them into space. The force of gravity makes the satellite fall toward Earth, but if the satellite is moving fast enough, it never gets any closer to Earth. It's falling around Earth instead.

Satellites gather helpful information. Will it rain today? The National Oceanic and Atmospheric Administration (NOAA) satellites give us a look at Earth's weather. Are you taking a trip? The Global Positioning System (GPS) is a network of 31 satellites that gives location information to the navigation systems in our cars and phones.

NASA satellites help us study the oceans, land, atmosphere, and outer space. One of them, the Hubble Space Telescope, orbits above the world's atmosphere, taking incredible space photos.

International Space Station

* *Sixteen nations worked together to build the International Space Station (ISS).*
* *The ISS orbits Earth every 90 minutes.*
* *Astronauts take turns living and working on it.*

The United States and 15 other nations built a space laboratory called the International Space Station (ISS). It orbits 250 miles above the earth and travels about 17,500 miles per hour!

Construction of the ISS began in 1998. The first crew of three astronauts arrived in November 2000. Since then, the space station has had people living there every day.

The ISS is made up of 15 pressurized modules, and each resembles a giant can. It has two bathrooms, a gymnasium, and a dome-like window so the astronauts can view Earth. Six robotic arms outside the station help with experiments, maintenance, and adding new modules.

Friction with the outer edge of Earth's atmosphere gradually slows the space station's orbit, so it will eventually spiral down to Earth. But don't worry—much of it will burn up on the way down. And a controlled return will let scientists make sure the remaining debris lands in a safe location.

Astronauts at Work

✳ Astronauts have a strict schedule without much playtime.
✳ They conduct experiments and repair equipment on the ISS.
✳ They're working on a plan to travel to Mars!

It may sound fun to be an astronaut, but these "star sailors" work many hours under challenging conditions. On the International Space Station (ISS), they go on spacewalks to repair equipment. They also conduct experiments in the ISS's low-gravity environment.

One cool experiment involves a robot. Using special technology, an astronaut can control this space helper just by moving his own body the way he wants the robot to move. The robot can do some of the riskier jobs so the astronaut doesn't have to.

Other experiments help astronauts prepare for a trip to Mars. For example, NASA is working on an expandable shelter called the Bigelow Expandable Activity Module (BEAM). This shelter collapses like a Slinky because space habitats must be lightweight and easy to set up. They also need to offer protection from solar radiation and space debris.

Far-Out Fact: Astronauts train for spacewalks in a swimming pool because floating in space is like floating in water.

Astronaut Profile

✴ *Colonel Jeffrey Williams completed four space missions.*

✴ *He spent 534 cumulative days in space and took over 330,000 space photos.*

✴ *He believes that true science agrees with Scripture.*

After four missions to the International Space Station (ISS), Col. Williams' favorite view from space is still Earth—he never gets tired of it! And he believes that everything he sees is part of God's special creation. In an interview with the Institute for Creation Research, Col. Williams said, "I don't find a conflict with true science—genuine science with integrity—and the Scriptures."

Part of an astronaut's job is doing spacewalks—leaving the ISS in a spacesuit to maintain the station or repair equipment. According to Col. Williams, "The preparations leading up to a spacewalk are pretty intense, the details are many...the tasks...are difficult, the unknowns are lurking, and the whole world is watching. The body gets pretty bruised and sore. But the rewards are great."

Col. Williams has spent decades furthering our knowledge of outer space, and he remains committed to the truth of God's creation. How can you help people learn about our amazing Creator?

Searching for Life

✶ So far, life has not been found on other planets.
✶ The Bible doesn't say God created life anywhere else.
✶ All life comes from God (Psalm 36:9).

The Bible doesn't tell us God created living beings anywhere but on Earth. But many Big Bang scientists continue the Search for Extraterrestrial Intelligence (SETI). They believe that life can evolve from non-living materials if the conditions are right.

A planet that orbits a star outside our solar system is known as an exoplanet. To support life, it must be similar to Earth. The exoplanet needs to orbit at the right distance from its star to create the right temperatures for liquid water. And its star has to be stable like our sun—no sudden, massive radiation flashes.

If an exoplanet is much smaller than Earth, it can't hold an atmosphere. Its atmosphere must have ozone, just enough oxygen, and lots of water. Even if an exoplanet met these requirements, it wouldn't mean that life could evolve there. Though water, oxygen, and chemicals support life, they attack the building blocks of life that aren't already part of a living being. Life comes from God.

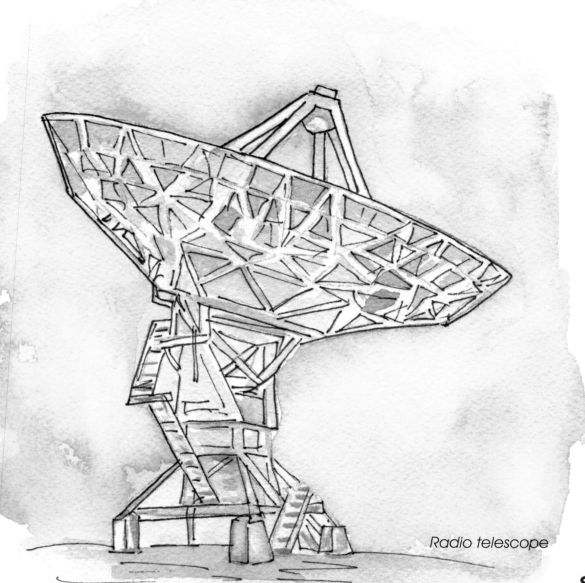

Radio telescope

Clearly Seen

* *The universe reveals some awesome things about God.*
* *Creation suffers under sin's curse.*
* *Jesus died to pay for our sins and give us a new life with Him.*

We've learned much about the universe in this small book. But what can the universe teach us about God? We see God's wisdom in how He made Earth an ideal place for life, placing it at the perfect location in our solar system. We see how He provides for us when the sun gives us light and warmth and as our planet supplies food, air, and water. The vastness of the universe gives us a glimpse of His power as we marvel that He spoke it all into being.

Yes, God's attributes are clearly seen in all that He has made (Romans 1:20).

As amazing as this universe is, it still suffers under sin's curse. Sin affects all of creation—especially people. Yet, we see God's love in what He did for us through His Son, Jesus. Our Creator, the Lord Jesus Christ, performed the greatest act of love when He came to Earth as a man. He lived a sinless life, died, and rose from the grave. His death served as payment for our

sinful hearts, and His resurrection allows us to live new lives.

For all who trust Him, He gives us a new life! And one day we will live with Him in a perfect new world—free to worship and enjoy our Creator forever. Will you trust and follow Him today?

Space Resources for Deeper Discovery

For more detailed answers to your space questions, visit ICR.org. Search for these articles and other news describing the latest scientific research. Space books and DVDs are offered in our online store (ICR.org/store).

Articles

"The Solar System" article series, Jason Lisle, Ph.D.

"Astronomers Speak: Our Solar System Is 'Special,'" Brian Thomas, M.S.

"Solar System Secrets Solved," Brian Thomas, M.S.

"Strong Evidence for Life on Mars?" Jake Hebert, Ph.D.

"Is the Universe Crowded with Earthlike Planets?" Frank Sherwin, M.A.

"Planet's Reverse Orbit a New Twist in Old Evolutionary Story," Brian Thomas, M.S.

"Pluto's Craterless Plains Look Young," Brian Thomas, M.S.

"The Hubble 'Pillars of Creation' Revisited," Jake Hebert, Ph.D.

"Did Astronomers Find an Evolving Planet?" Brian Thomas, M.S.

"Mythical Planet Doesn't Solve Orbit Origins," Brian Thomas, M.S.

"Wanted: Young Creation Scientists," Jake Hebert, Ph.D.

"Above All the Earth," an interview with NASA astronaut Col. Jeff Williams

Books

Guide to the Universe

Guide to Creation Basics

The Work of His Hands: A View of God's Creation from Space

The Solar System: God's Heavenly Handiwork, available through Kindle and NOOK

DVDs

The Universe: A Journey Through God's Grand Design

Astronomy Reveals Creation

What You Aren't Being Told About Astronomy, Volumes 1-3

Unlocking the Mysteries of Genesis, Episodes 1, 10, and 11

Glossary

Antimatter Particles having the same mass as normal matter but the opposite electrical charge.

Astronomical unit A unit of length equal to the approximate distance from Earth to the sun—93 million miles. It's used to measure distances within our solar system.

Atmosphere Layer of gases surrounding a planet or other celestial body.

Aurora Streams of colored light that stretch across the sky at the North and South Poles. They're caused by interaction between solar particles, Earth's atmosphere, and Earth's magnetic field.

Axis The imaginary straight line that a rotating planet or moon spins around.

Celestial objects Any objects located outside of Earth's atmosphere.

Centaur A small space object that orbits the sun between Jupiter and Neptune and crosses at least one gas giant's orbit. It displays characteristics of both an asteroid and a comet.

Cosmonaut A Russian astronaut.

Crater A large, rounded hole in the ground on the surface of a planet or moon. It's usually caused by the impact of a meteorite or other celestial body.

Dwarf planet A smaller celestial body that orbits around the sun like a planet but shares its orbit with nearby objects, some of which may affect the dwarf planet's orbit.

Energy The ability to do work.

Epicycles Part of Ptolemy's incorrect theory that the sun, moon, and planets orbit in small circles upon larger circles around the earth.

Exoplanet A planet that orbits a star other than our sun.

Firmament A word used in older English Bibles that refers to Earth's sky and outer space. It means the same thing as "the heavens."

Gravity An invisible force that pulls objects toward each other.

Heavens Earth's sky and space beyond.

Helium A colorless, odorless gas that is lighter than air.

Hubble Space Telescope NASA's telescope that orbits Earth and takes space photos.

Hydrogen A colorless, odorless, lightweight, highly flammable gas.

International Space Station (ISS) An orbiting laboratory built by 16 countries and manned by a rotating crew of astronauts and cosmonauts.

Light pollution Any negative effect of artificial light. One example is the way city lights hinder what we can see in the night sky.

Light-year A unit of length used to measure distances in space. It's equal to the distance light can travel in one year—5.88 trillion miles.

Magnetic field An invisible field produced by moving electrical charges that influence other moving charges.

Mass A measurement of the amount of matter in an object. The number, type, and density of its atoms determine an object's mass.

Matter Anything in the universe that has mass and takes up space.

Methane A colorless, odorless, flammable gas made of carbon and hydrogen.

Moon The natural satellite of Earth. Also used to describe natural satellites of other planets.

Orbit The path a space object travels around another, larger space object.

Orbital period The amount of time it takes a space object to travel all the way around another space object.

Ozone A molecule made up of three oxygen atoms. The ozone layer in our atmosphere protects life on Earth from most of the sun's harmful ultraviolet rays.

Parsec A unit of length used to measure long distances between Earth and space objects outside the solar system. One parsec equals 3.26 light-years or 19 trillion miles.

Physics A branch of science related to the God-given laws that govern matter, motion, and energy.

Planetary conjunction This occurs when two celestial bodies appear close to each other in Earth's sky.

Satellite A space object that orbits around another, larger space object.

Space probe Spacecraft used to gather information about outer space.

Solar flares Giant bursts of energy from the sun.

Solar particles High-energy charged particles emitted into space from the sun.

Solar radiation Energy emitted by the sun. Too much exposure can harm life.

Solar system The sun and all the objects orbiting around it.

Space The area beyond Earth's atmosphere.

Space debris Any man-made objects orbiting Earth that no longer serve a purpose—like broken satellites.

Spacewalk Any time an astronaut exits a vehicle while in space.

Supernova The gigantic explosion of a very massive star.

Trans-Neptunian objects Minor planets beyond Neptune's orbit in the solar system.

Trojan moon A moon that shares an orbit with another, larger moon, but they never collide because they travel at the same speed.

Universe Everything we can detect, sense, feel, touch, or measure.

Waning When less of the moon shines than the night before, and it looks like it's getting smaller.

Waxing When more of the moon shines than the night before, and it looks like it's getting bigger.

White hole This is a hypothetical area in space. While a black hole consumes light and energy as it grows, a white hole would force light and energy to escape as it shrinks. It would eventually disappear. Scientists have yet to discover a white hole.

Index

V-Z

Contributors

Susan Windsor is the graphic designer and illustrator for the Institute for Creation Research. Even though it was demoted to dwarf status, her favorite planet is still Pluto.

Christy Hardy is a writer and editor for ICR. She enjoys stargazing from the Eagle Eye Observatory in Burnet, Texas. Her favorite planet is Jupiter.

Truett Billups is a writer and editor for ICR. He enjoys playing chess, and his favorite celestial object is asteroid B-612.

Michael Stamp is a writer and editor for ICR. He also writes Christian novels. His favorite moon is Jupiter's Io.

Brian Thomas is a science researcher, writer, and presenter for ICR. He is an expert in biotechnology and dino soft tissues. He really likes comet Hartley-2. It shoots jets.

Jayme Durant is the Director of Communications and Executive Editor for ICR. Her favorite planet is Earth because there's nothing quite like home sweet home.

Thank You

A special thank you to Dr. Jake Hebert and Dr. Vernon Cupps for their careful review of this book. Their expertise in physics and knowledge of astronomy proved invaluable as we sought to accurately represent ICR's commitment to solid science and biblical creation.

We'd also like to thank ICR's CEO Dr. Henry M. Morris III for his support throughout the development of this project, his biblical expertise, and his thorough review of this book.

As with all of our projects, we want to express deep appreciation for others in the Communications Department at ICR: Beth Mull, Senior Editor, provided her seasoned expertise in reviewing and editing this book, and James Turner and Michael Hansen provided input along the way.

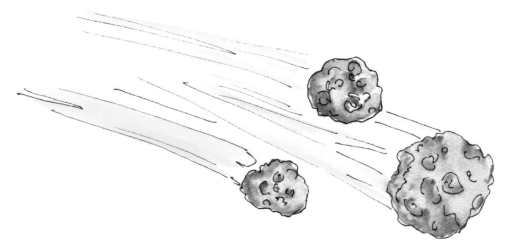

About ICR

At the Institute for Creation Research, we want you to know God's Word can be trusted with everything it speaks about—from how and why we were made, to how the universe was formed, to how we can know God and receive all He has planned for us.

To build your faith, our scientists have spent decades researching how science confirms what the Bible says. Our experts earned degrees in many different fields, including genetics, biotechnology, astronomy, astrophysics, physics, nuclear physics, zoology, geology, medicine, public health, theology, and engineering.

In addition to our books, we publish a monthly *Acts & Facts* magazine, a quarterly *Days of Praise* devotional, and loads of scientific articles online. We also produce DVD series on science and the Bible, and our scientists travel across the country to speak at events and share their findings. Follow us on Facebook @ICRscience and Twitter @ICRscience for current ICR news. For more information on our ministry, please visit our website, ICR.org.